THE BOOK OF LOVE AND WISDOM

CHRISTINE HAAS

Print information available on the last page

Rev. date: 11/21/2016

To order additional copies of this book, contact:
Xlibris
1-800-455-039
www.xlibris.com.au
Orders@Xlibris.com.au

PREFACE:

This book, my first prototype, illustrated with my Spiritual drawings, is dedicated to my helpers and guides and, for all my friends and supporters.

The small text under the pictures, is a reference to the meaning of my drawings, along with the path of my Spiritual awakening.

Love is All that is, for it is from my heart Chakra that the Divine Light shines.

Namaste

A book of Love and Wisdom for all.

Blessings

DEAR ARCHANGEL MICHAEL, PLEASE COME TO ME NOW, I NEED YOUR HELP

AND AN OWL BETWEEN THE WORLDS FLEW TO PROTECT US

I SAW AN ANGEL

IN THE FOREST

AND ALL LIT UP

SHE WAS LOOKING
AT THE BUTTERFLY:
TRANSFORMATION

AND THE DAWN OF
A NEW DAY ROSE
UPON THE EARTH

SO I PRAYED AND
JESUS HEARD

THE POWER OF
PRAYER WHERE
INTENTION GOES,
ENERGY GOES

MOTHER EARTH
HEARD MY PRAY
AND WOKE

SHE OPENED MY EYES AND SHOWED ME THE WAY OF THE FAIRY

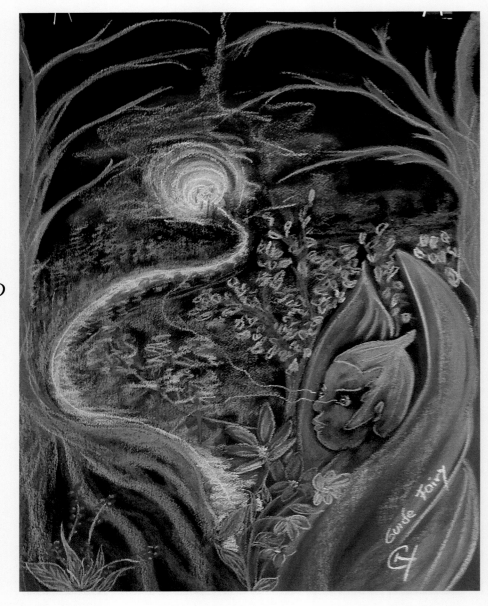

AND IT OPENED
THE GATE OF
THE GARDEN
OF MY HEART

SO I COULD SEE THE FES, THE FAIRIES, AND THE EARTH ANGELS KINGDOM

AND SO THE
NATURE SPIRITS

*HIDDEN IN THE
FOREST AND FROM
THE NATURAL EYES*

THEN MERLIN,
THE MASTER
OF ALL MAGIC
SHOWED HIMSELF

*WITH THE DRAGON
OF LIGHT*

*SO ALL THE SHAMANS
OF THE WORLD PRAYED
IN CEREMONIAL*

*THE AMERINDIANS
SHAMANS, THE
AFRICANS, THE
AUSTRALIANS,
THE RUSSIANS
SHAMANS, ALL OF THEM
TO SAVE THE EARTH*

*AND THE PROPHECY
CAME TO FRUITION*

THE NEW TRUTH IS OUT, SO BARAMAY CALLED

A NEW EARTH
NEW ENERGIES

RAISE YOUR ENERGY, JOY

UNTIL THE RAISE
OF THE JAGUAR

THE END

Printed in the United States
By Bookmasters